Hi Kids,

Welcome to the 1, 2, 3's of Golf.
Give me a **"WOOF WOOF"** for Marvin!

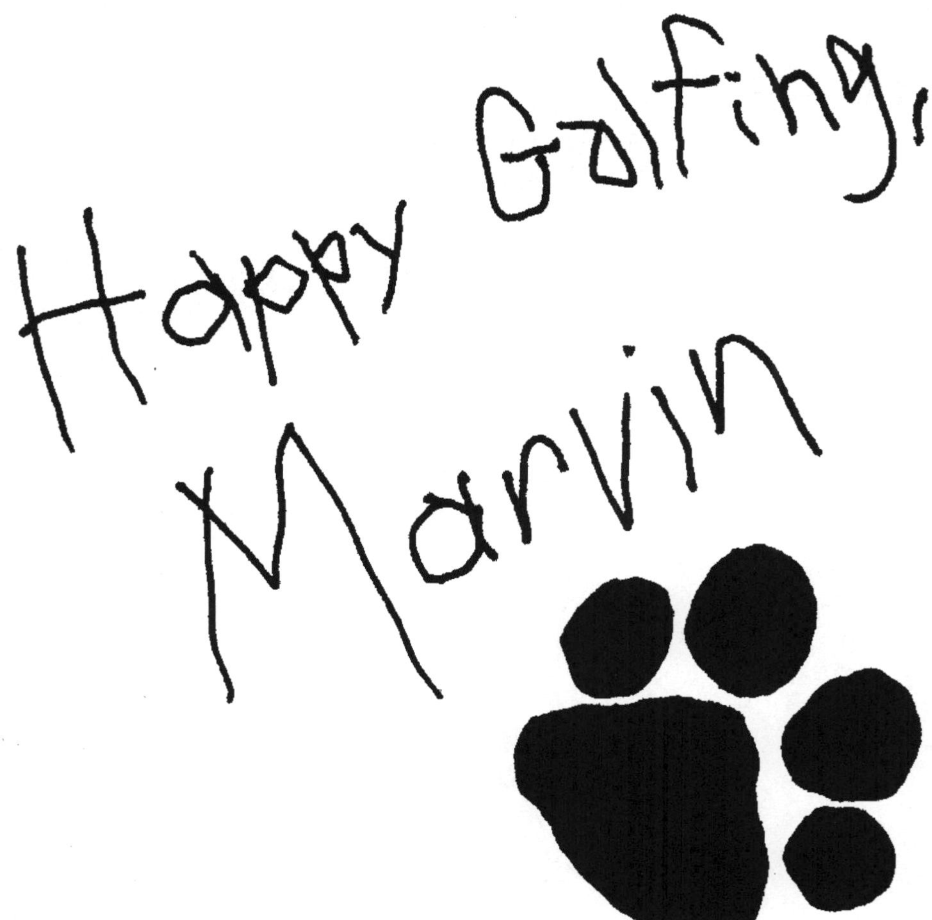

A special thank you to Jill Mann Strite for helping me "*putt*" this book together.

Illustrations by Bob Allen

Published by Mann USA, Inc.
Omaha, NE 68144
www.thebookmann.com

ISBN: 978-0-9797322-2-5

Library of Congress data on file with the publisher

Printed in the United States of America

10 9 8 7 6 5 4 3 2 1

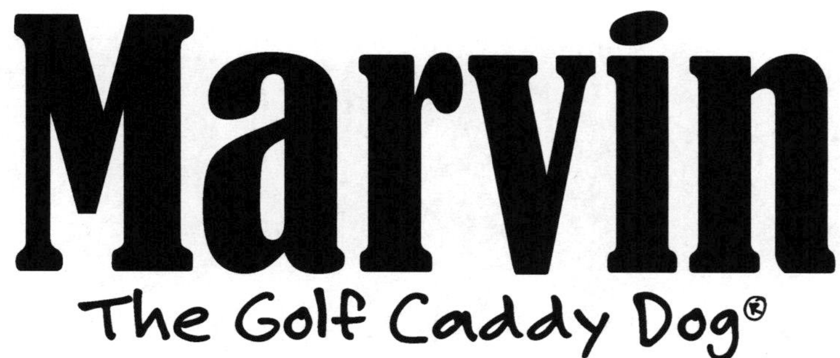

1, 2, 3's of Golf

Harold R. Mann
Illustrated by Bob Allen

Mann USA, Inc.

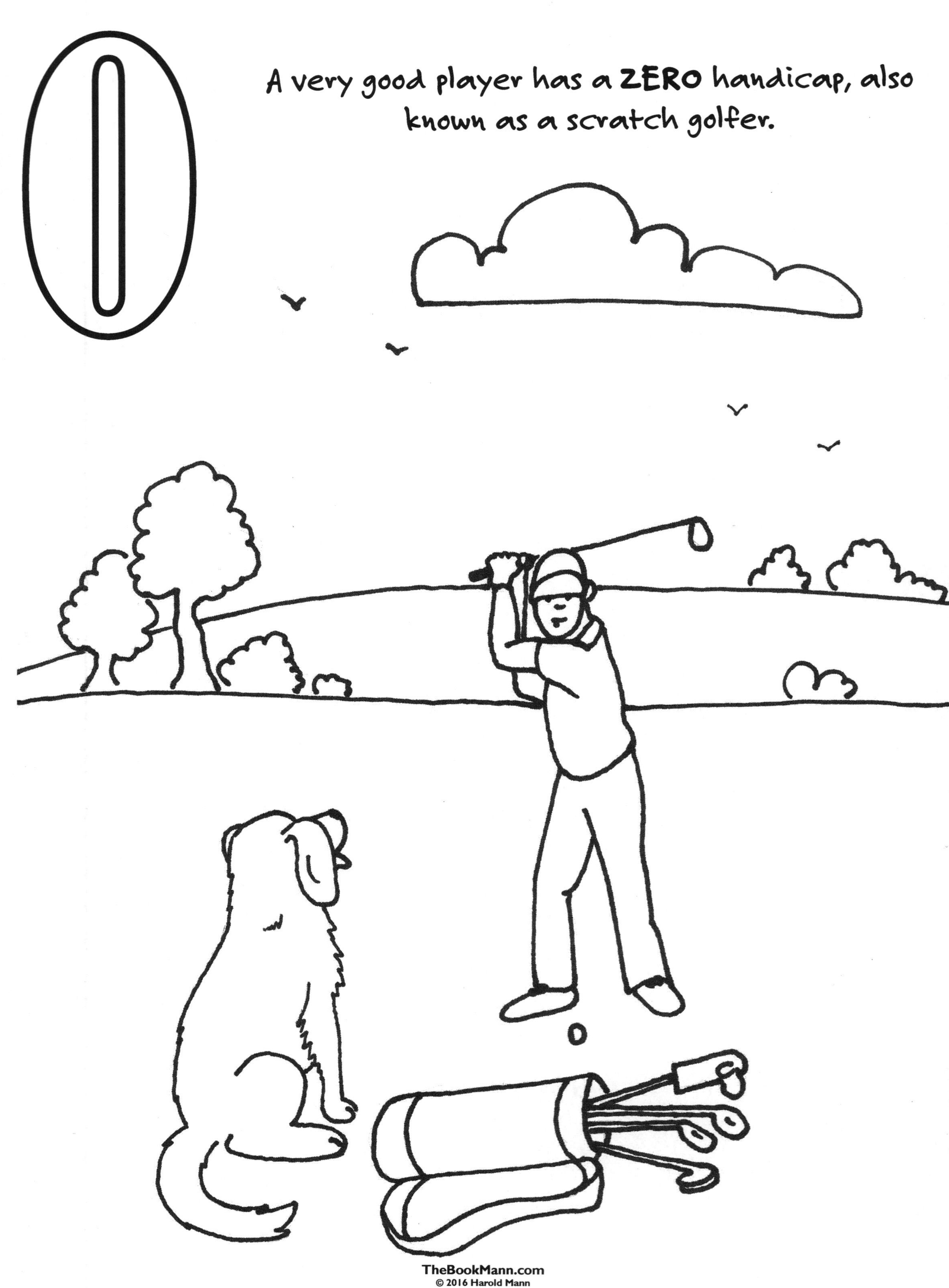

TheBookMann.com

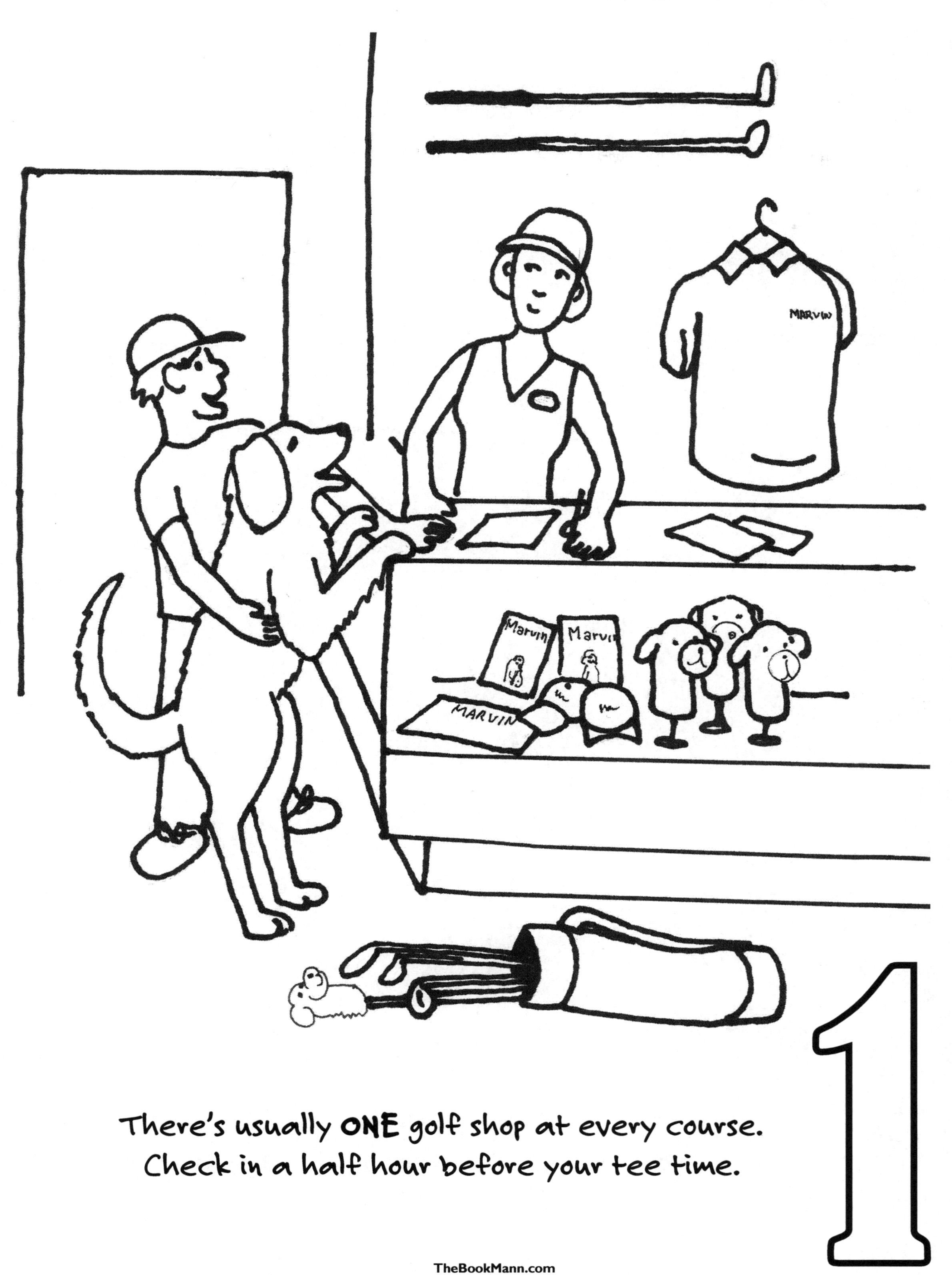

There's usually **ONE** golf shop at every course.
Check in a half hour before your tee time.

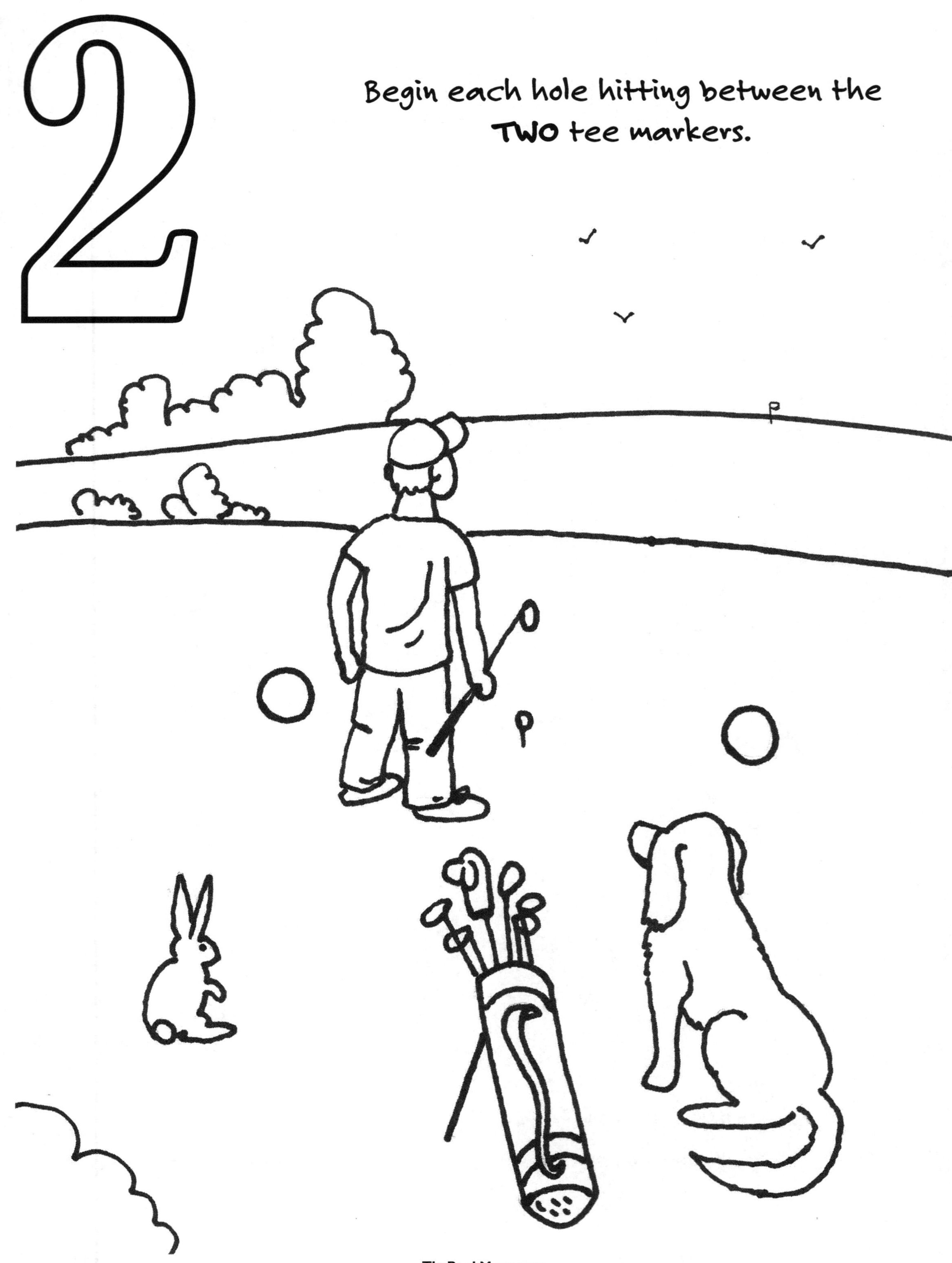
2
Begin each hole hitting between the
TWO tee markers.
TheBookMann.com

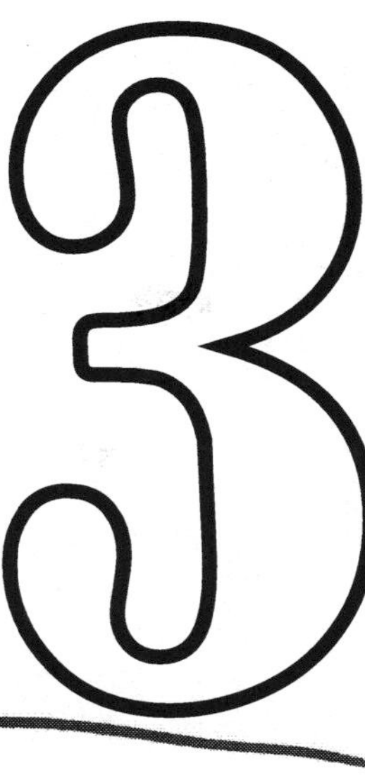

There are **THREE** golf balls in a sleeve.

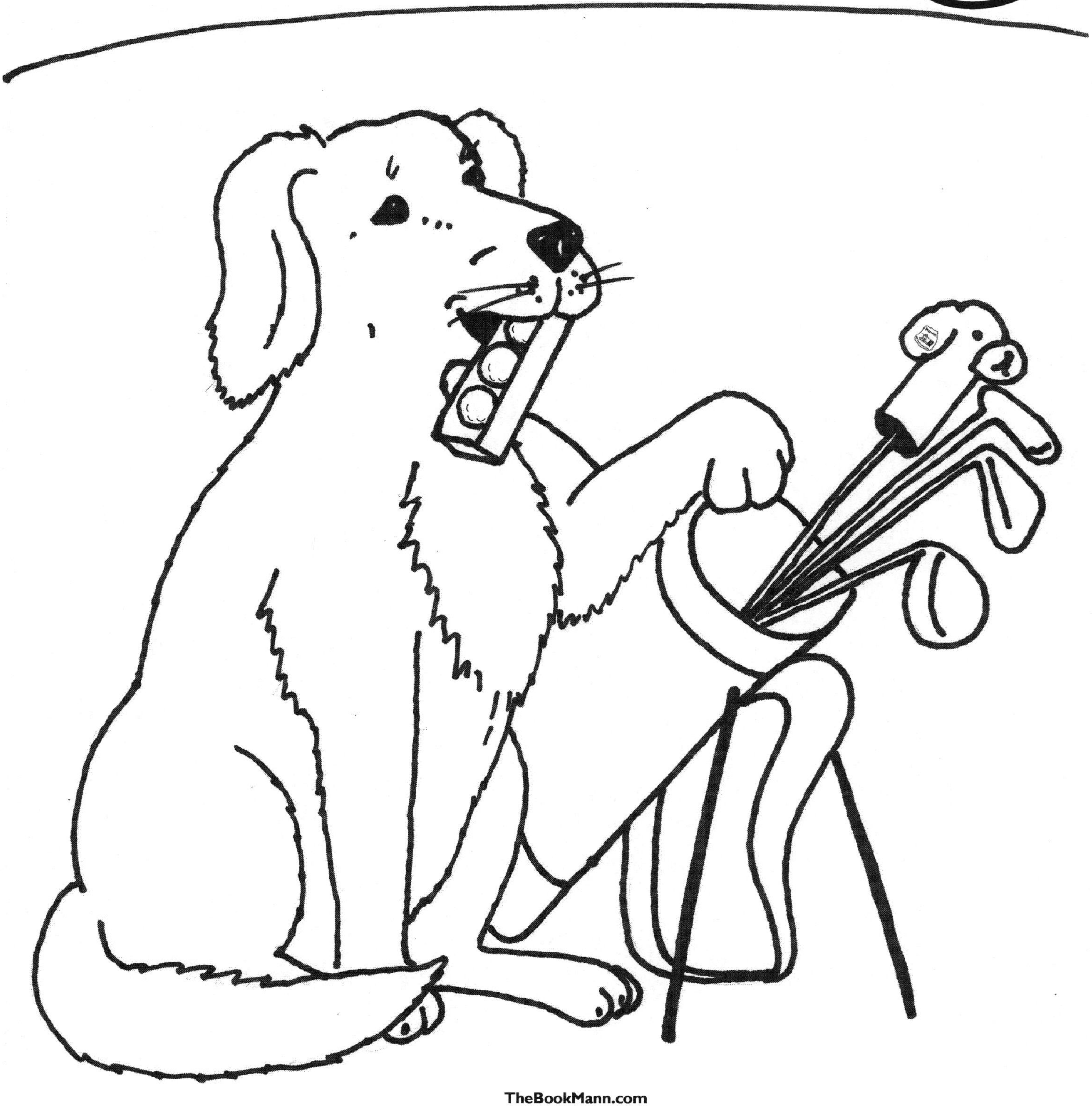

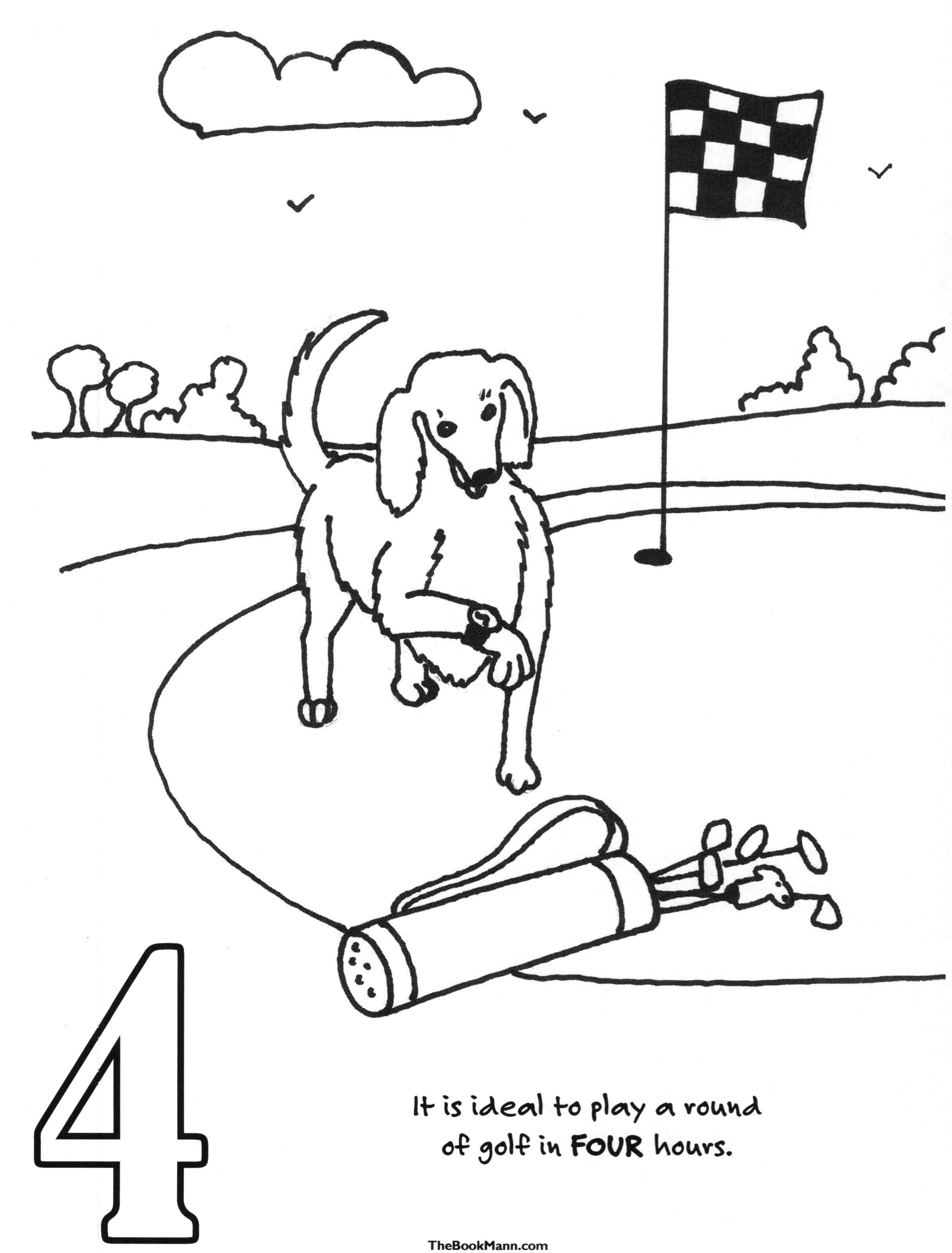
4
It is ideal to play a round
of golf in FOUR hours.
TheBookMann.com

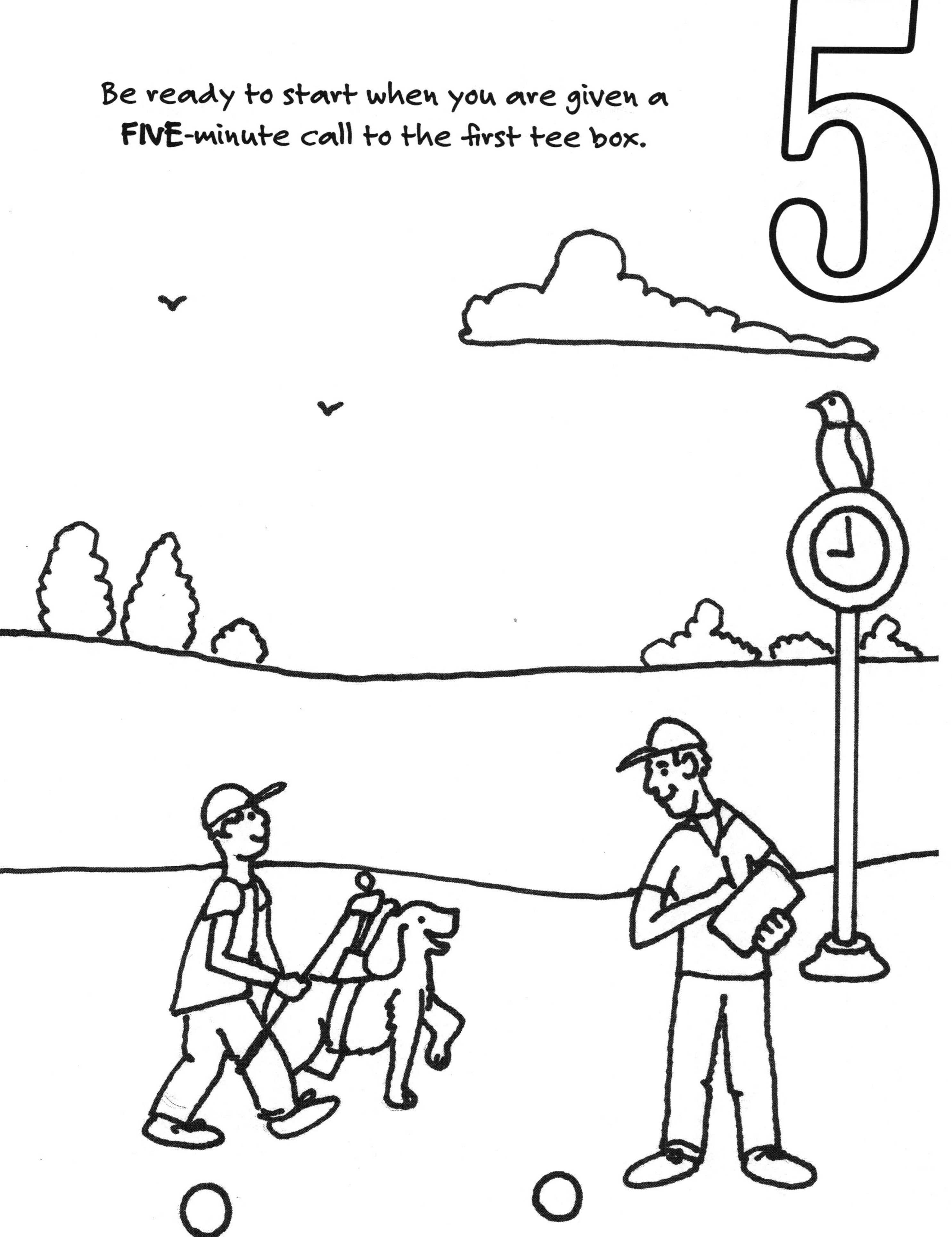
5
Be ready to start when you are given a
FIVE-minute call to the first tee box.

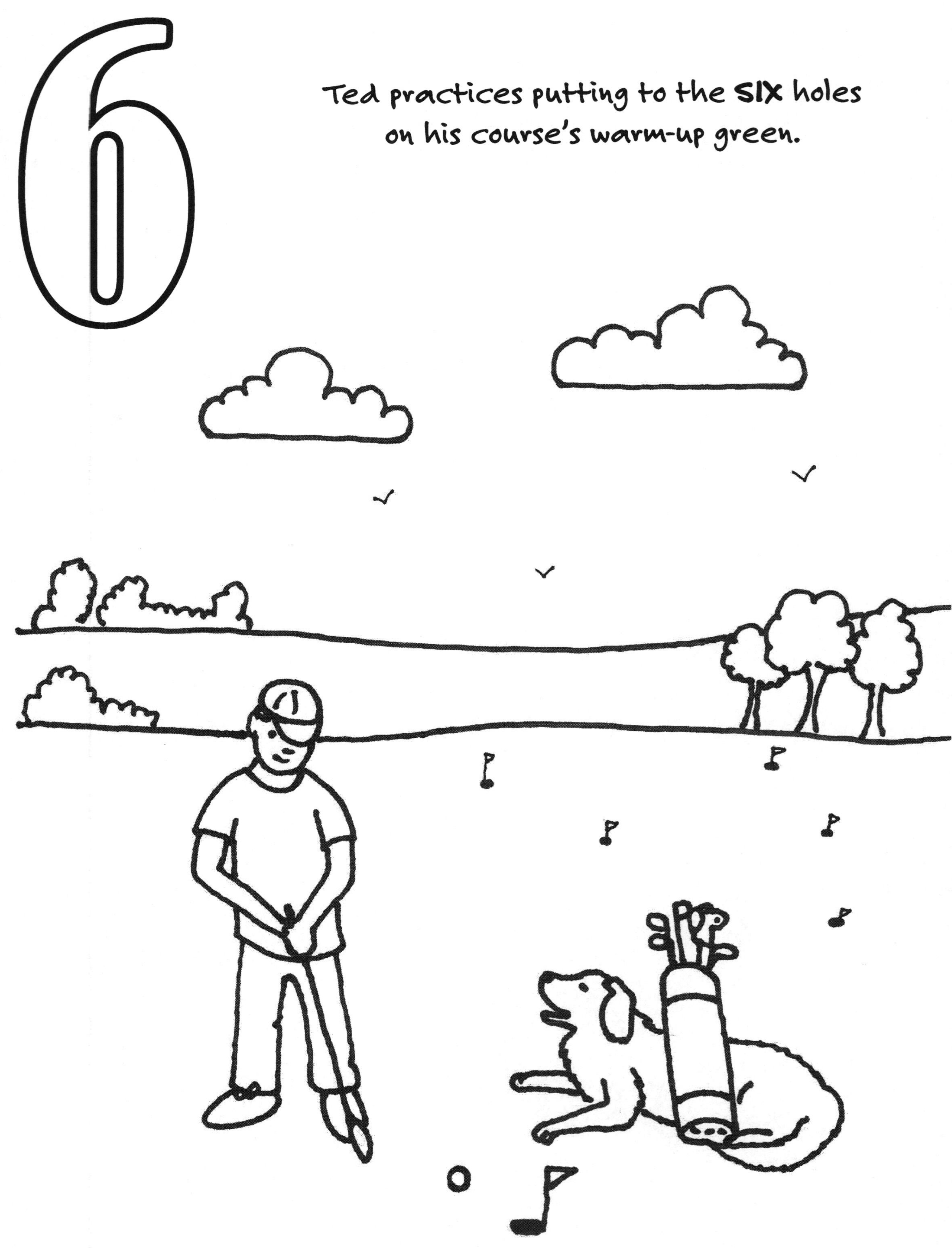

6

Ted practices putting to the **SIX** holes on his course's warm-up green.

Ted hits to all **SEVEN** targets on the driving range before teeing off.

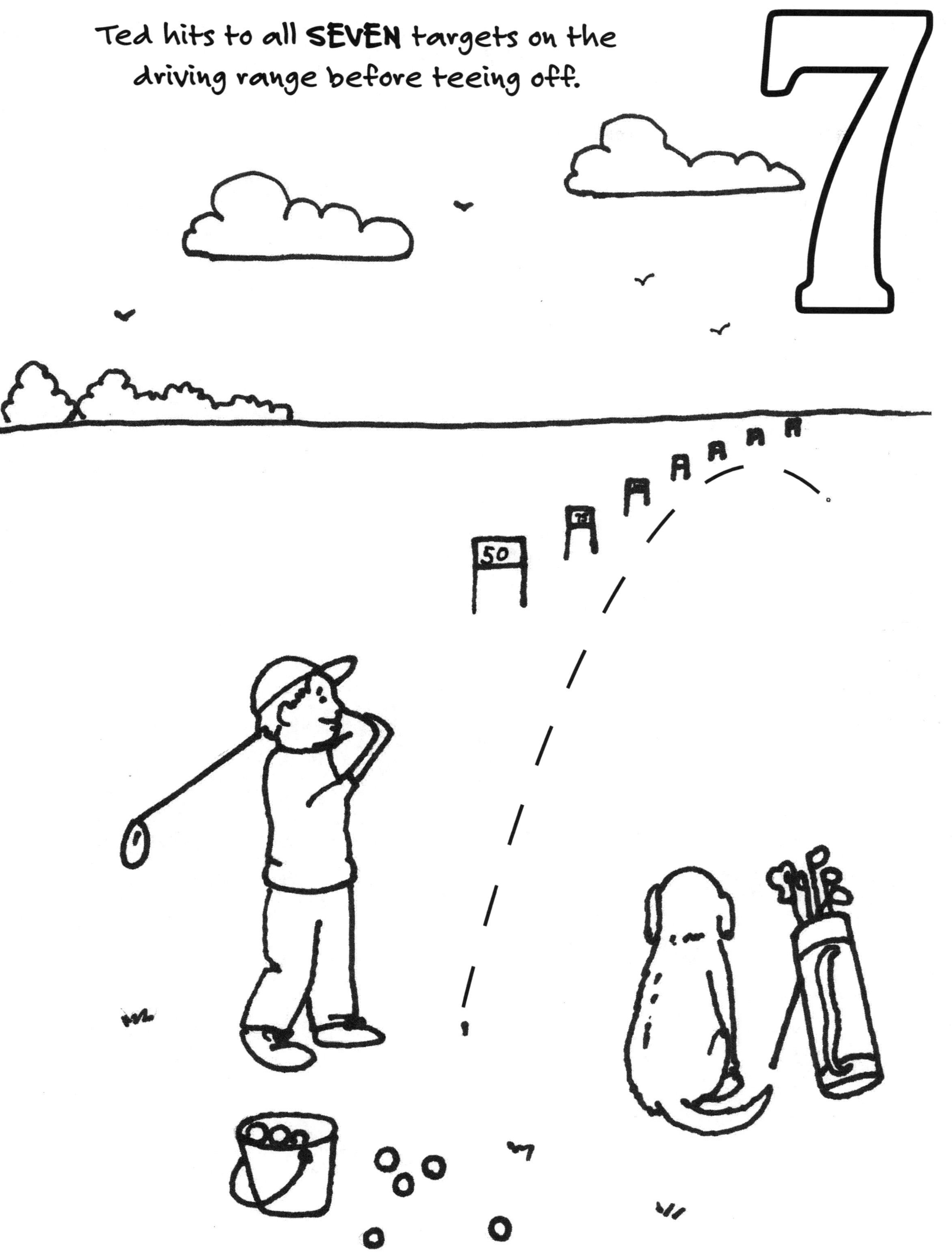

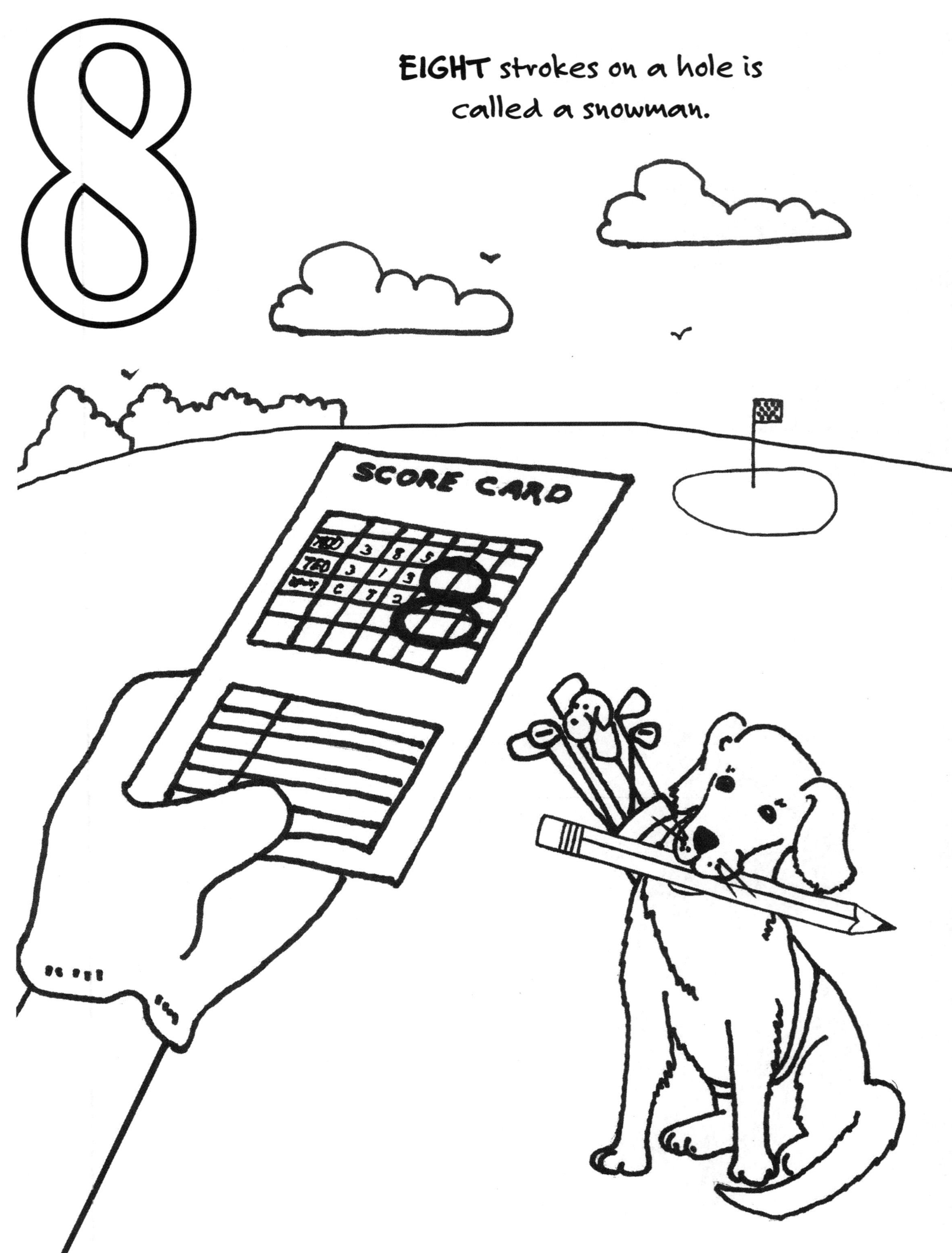
8
EIGHT strokes on a hole is
called a snowman.
SCORE CARD

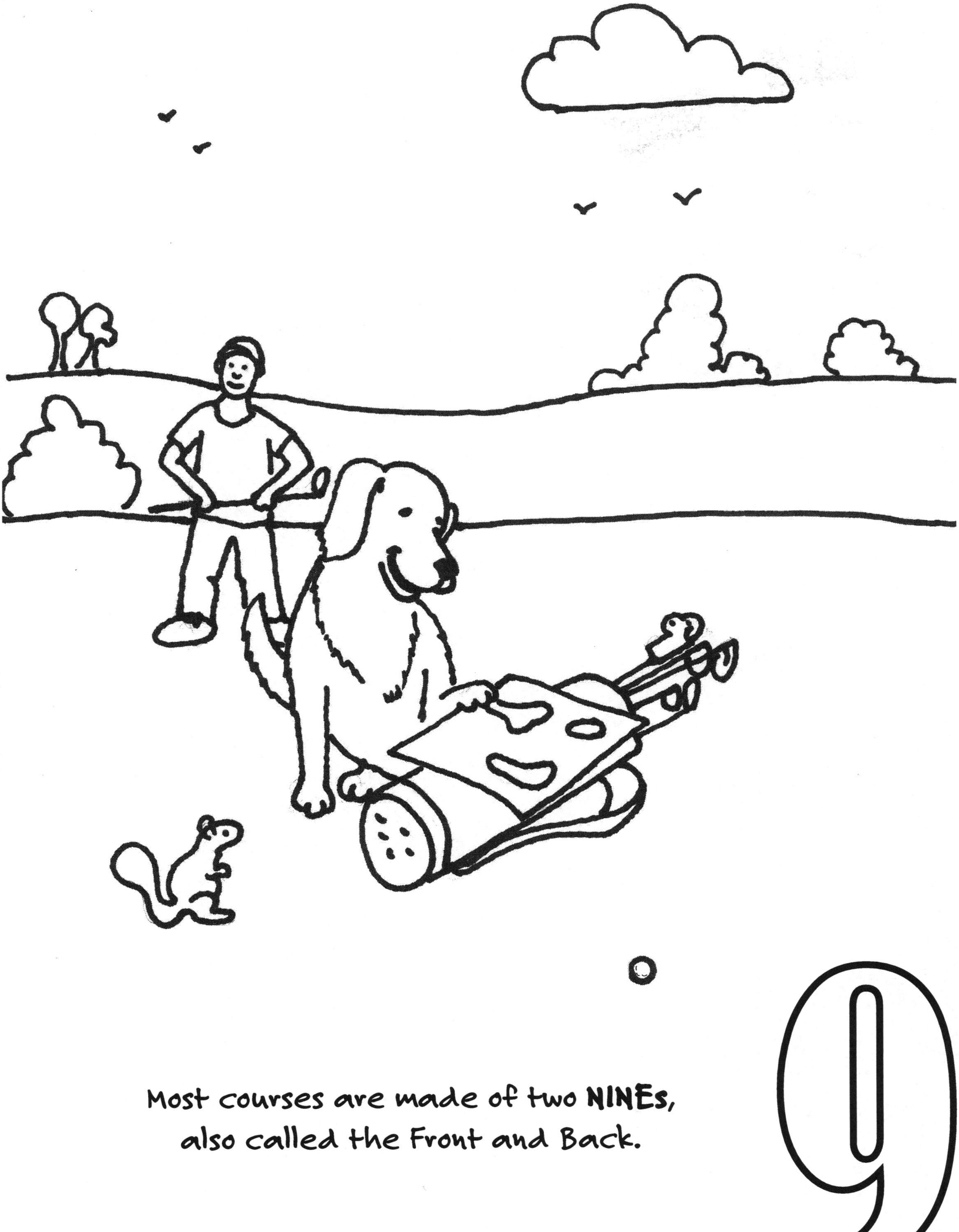

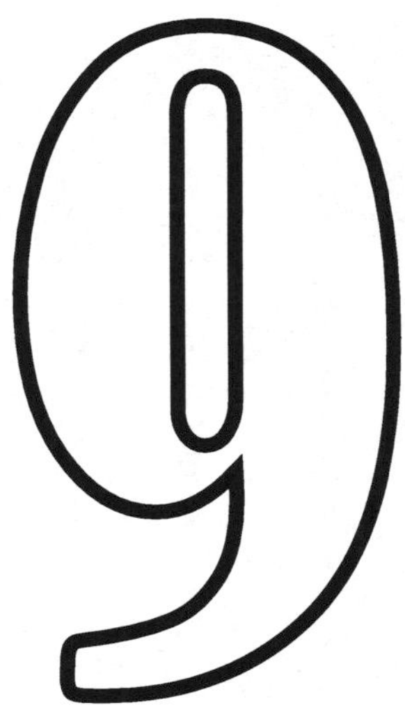

Most courses are made of two **NINEs**, also called the Front and Back.

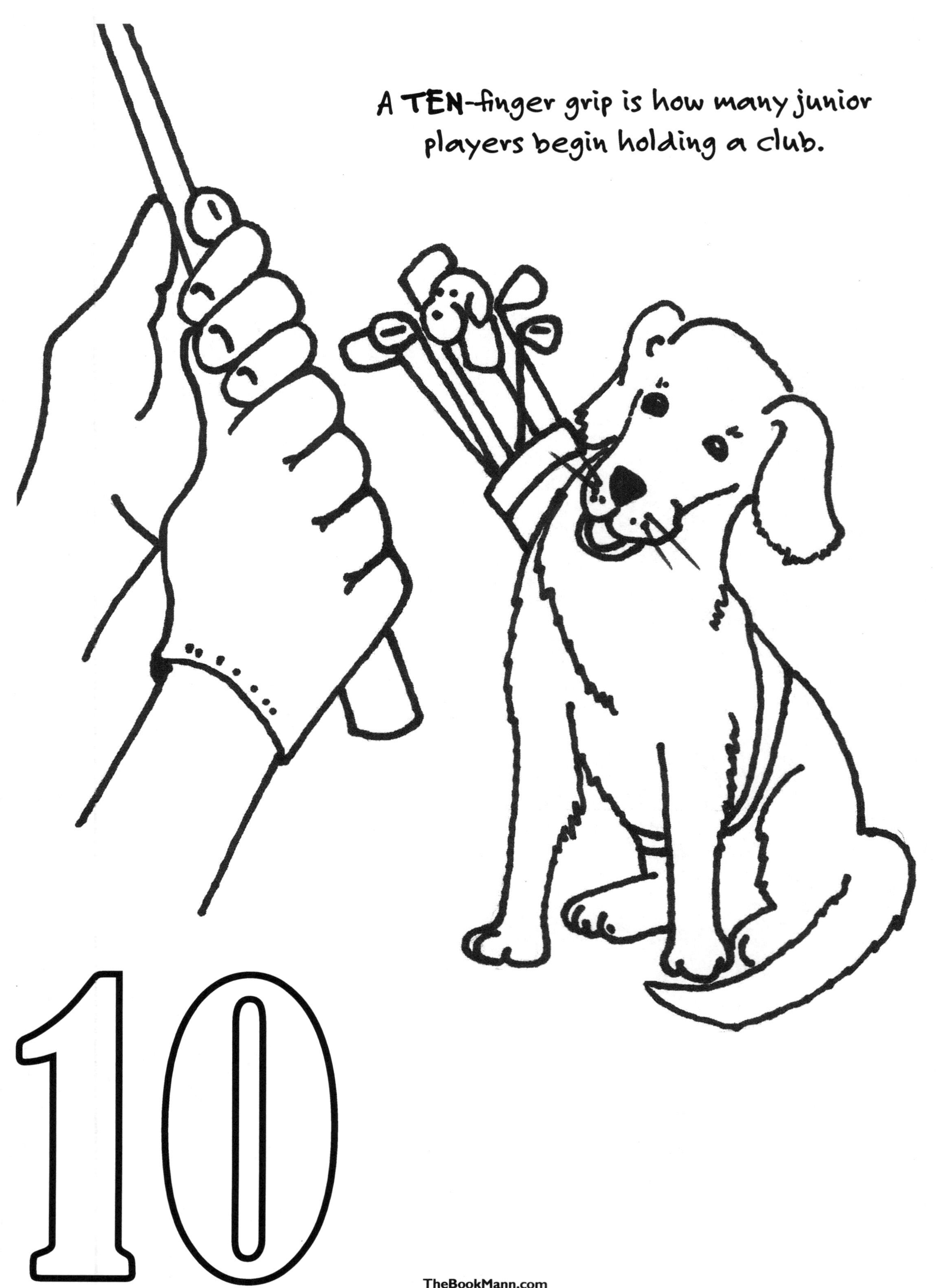
A TEN-finger grip is how many junior players begin holding a club.
10

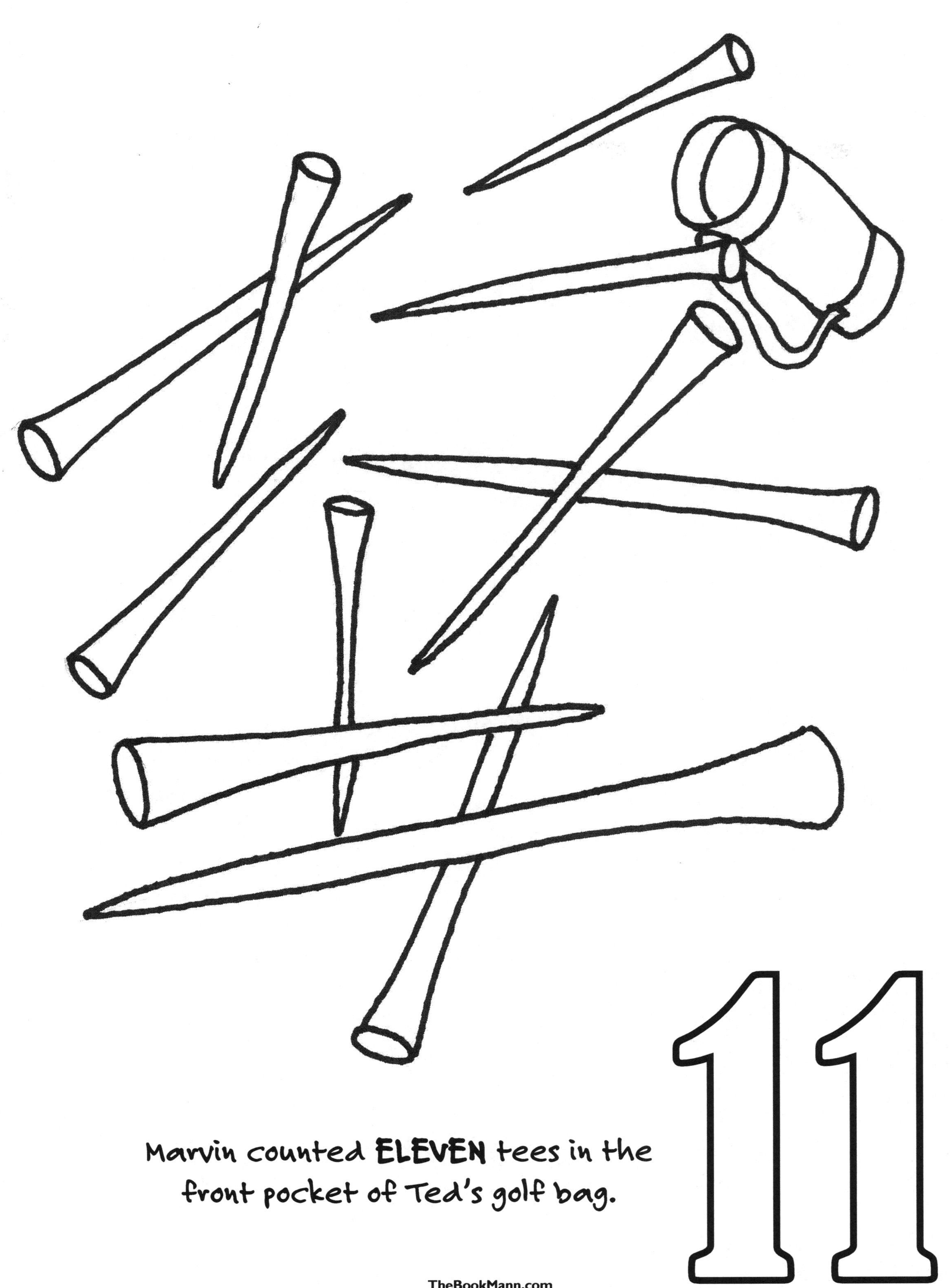

Marvin counted **ELEVEN** tees in the front pocket of Ted's golf bag.

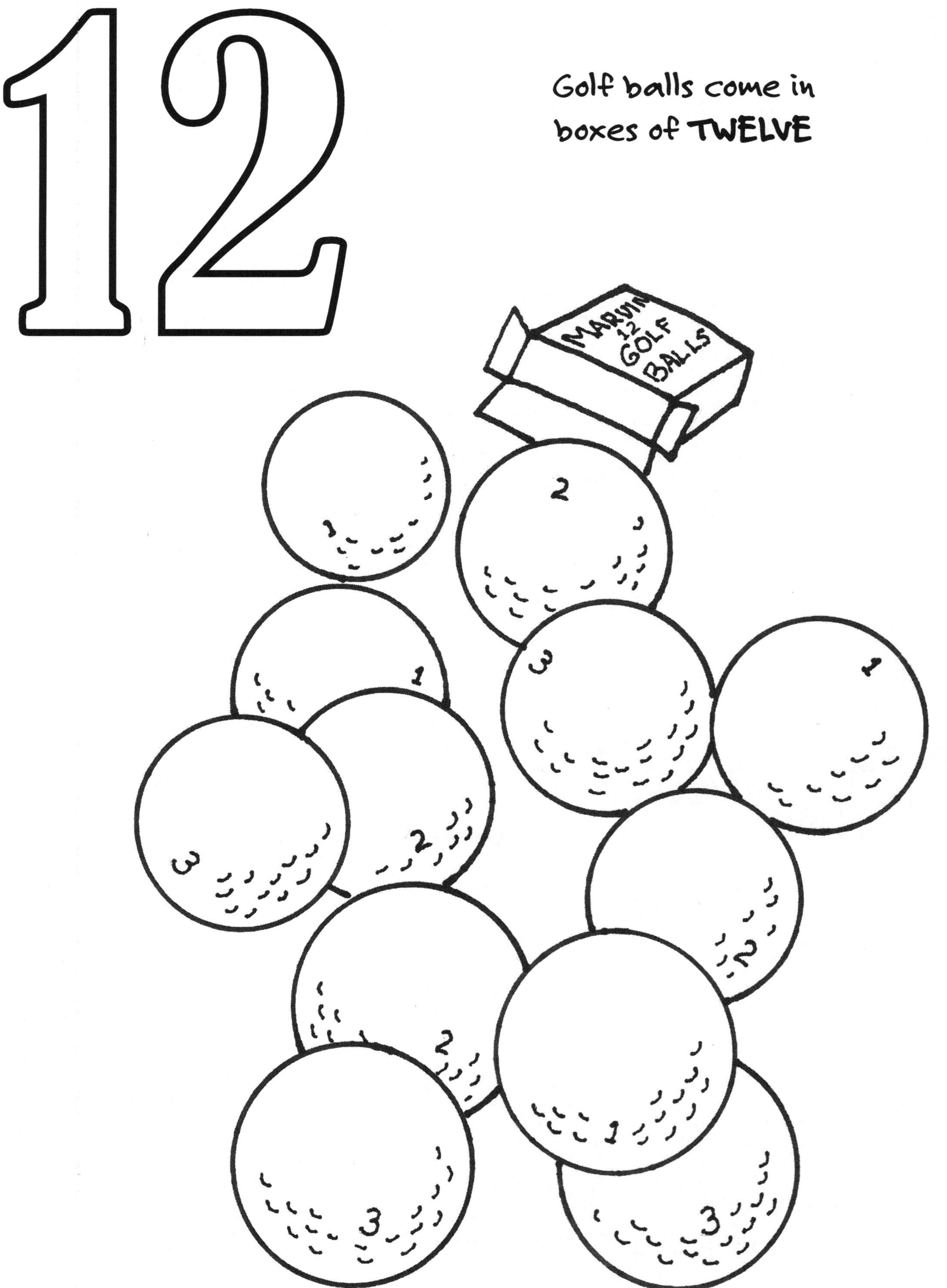

Golf balls come in boxes of **TWELVE**

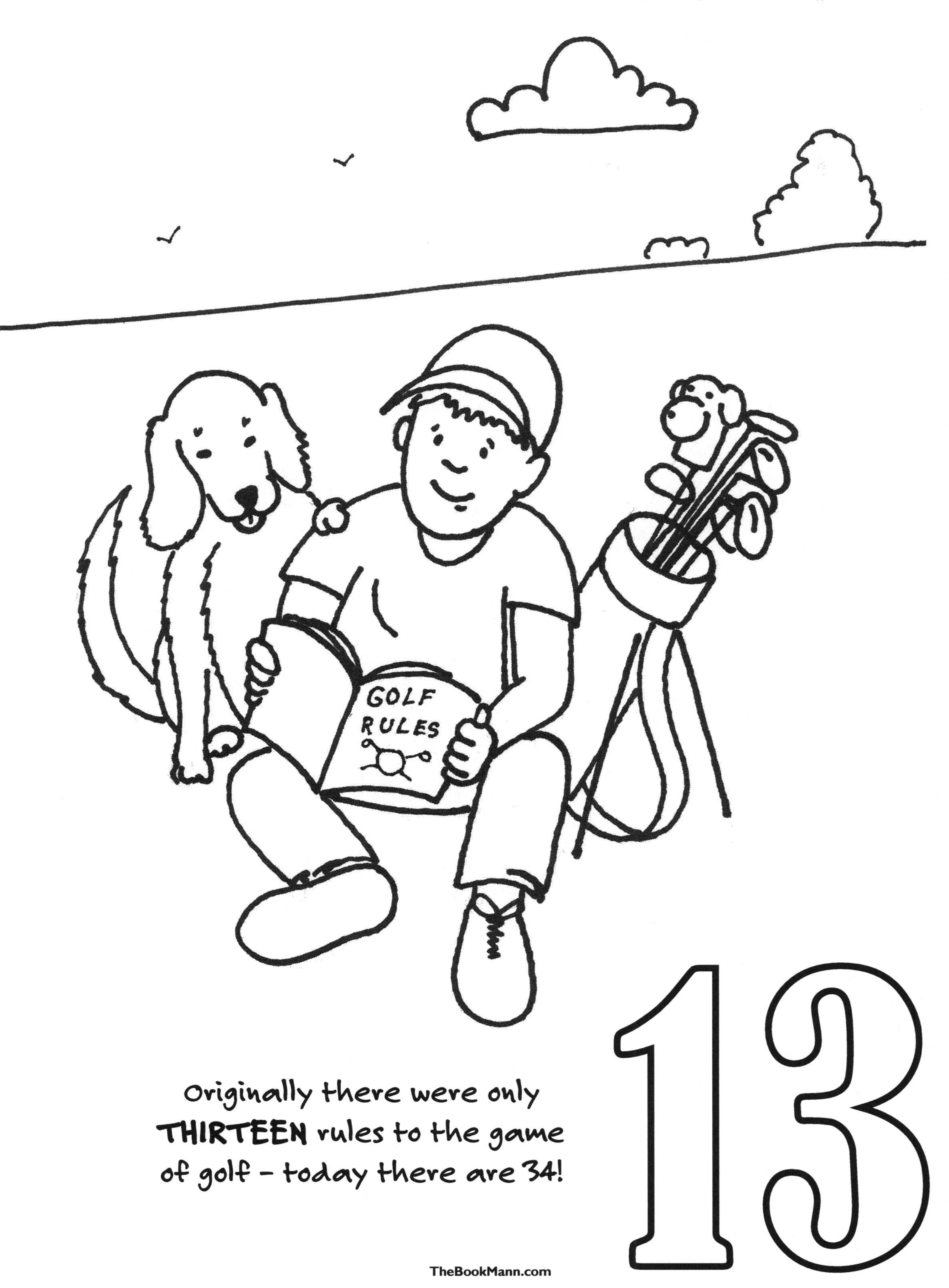

Originally there were only **THIRTEEN** rules to the game of golf – today there are 34!

14

Always check to be sure there are no more than **FOURTEEN** clubs in your golf bag.

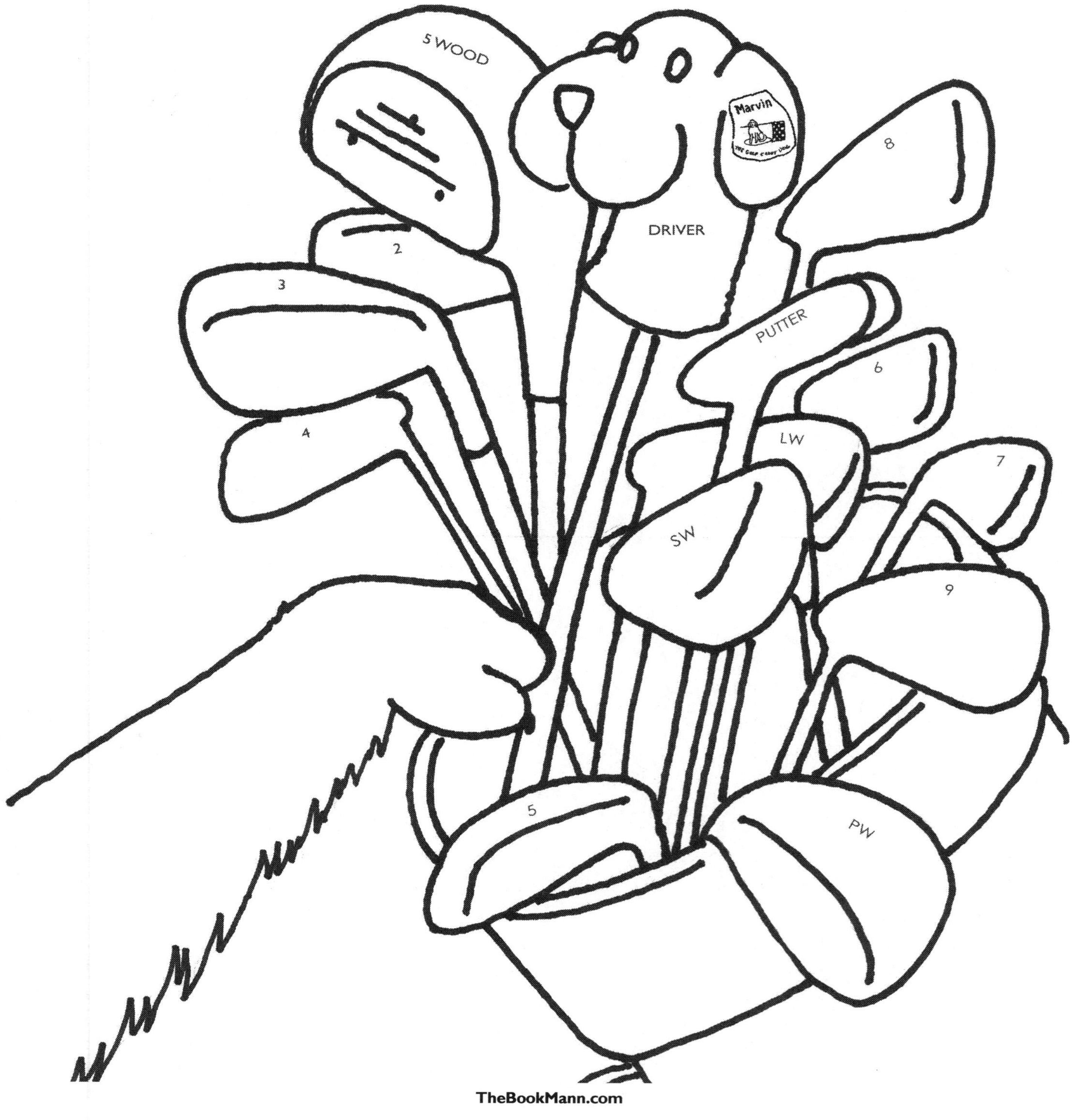

15

A ball retriever is also known as the **FIFTEENTH** club.

16

Keep hydrated by drinking at least **SIXTEEN** ounces of water.

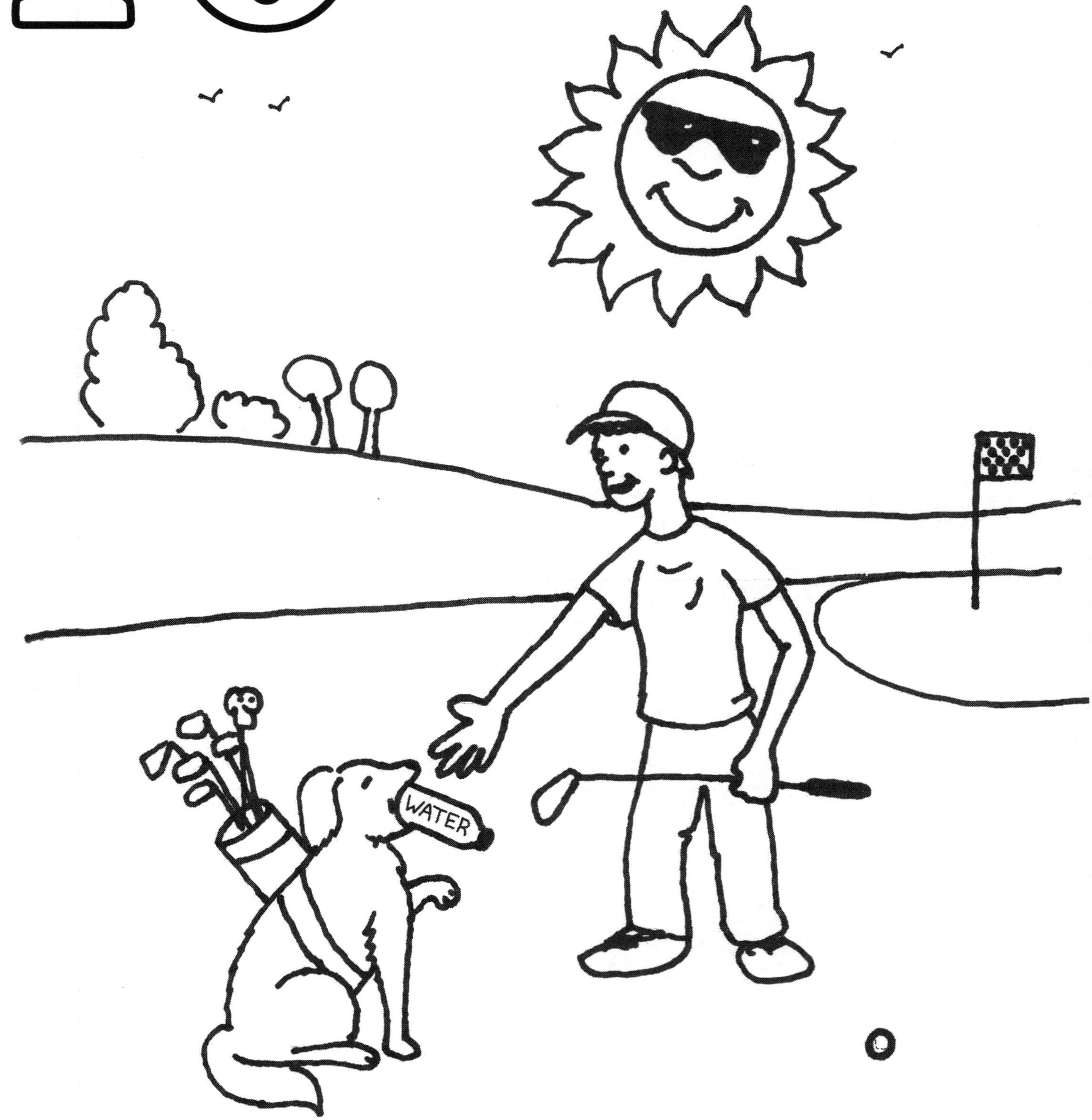

WATER

17

Rule **SEVENTEEN** includes everything you need to know about the Flagstick.

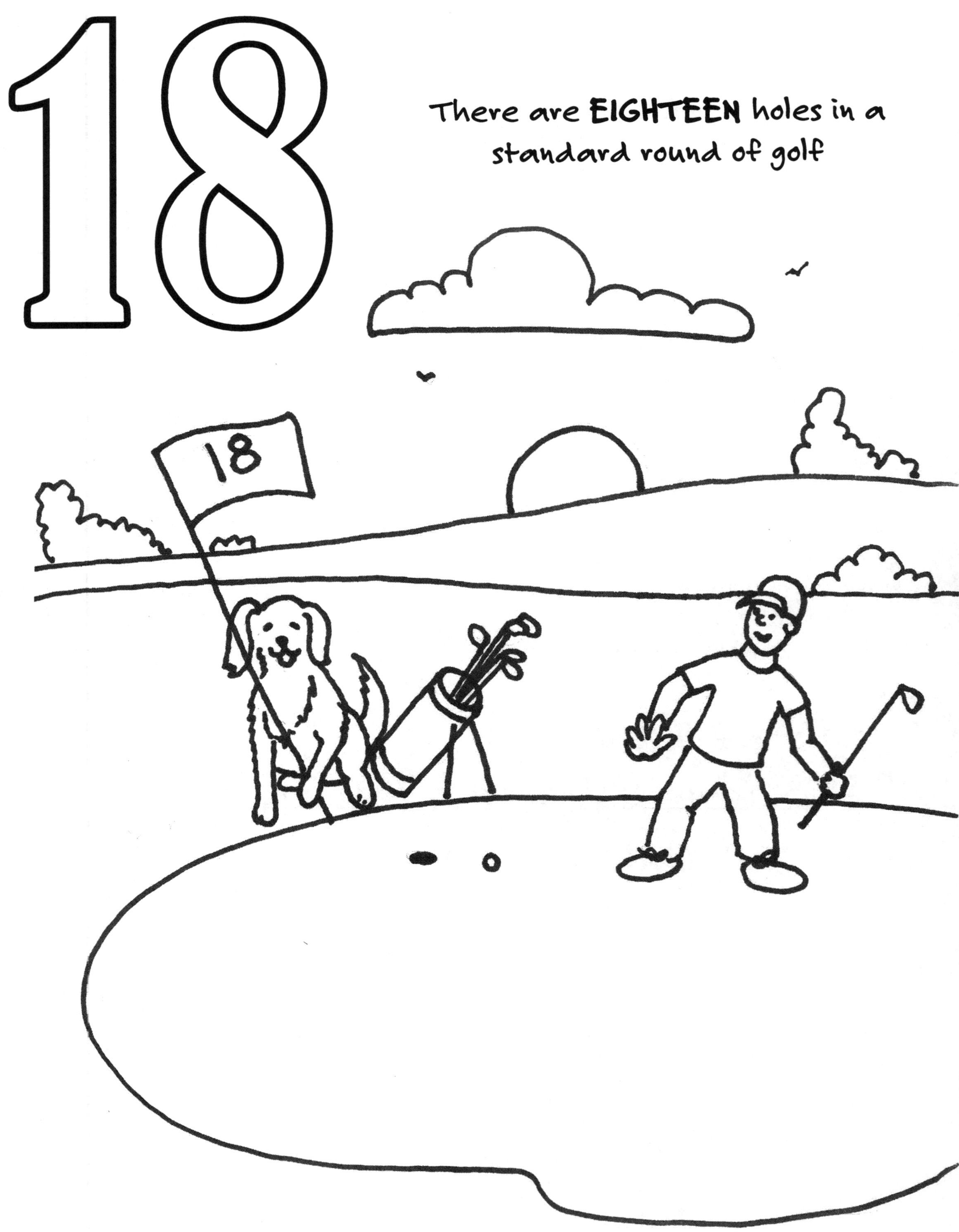
18
There are **EIGHTEEN** holes in a standard round of golf
18

Enjoy a meal after your round in the **NINETEENTH** Hole Café.

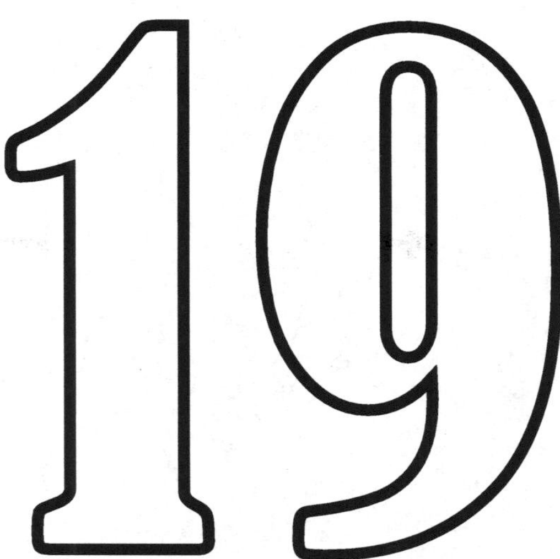

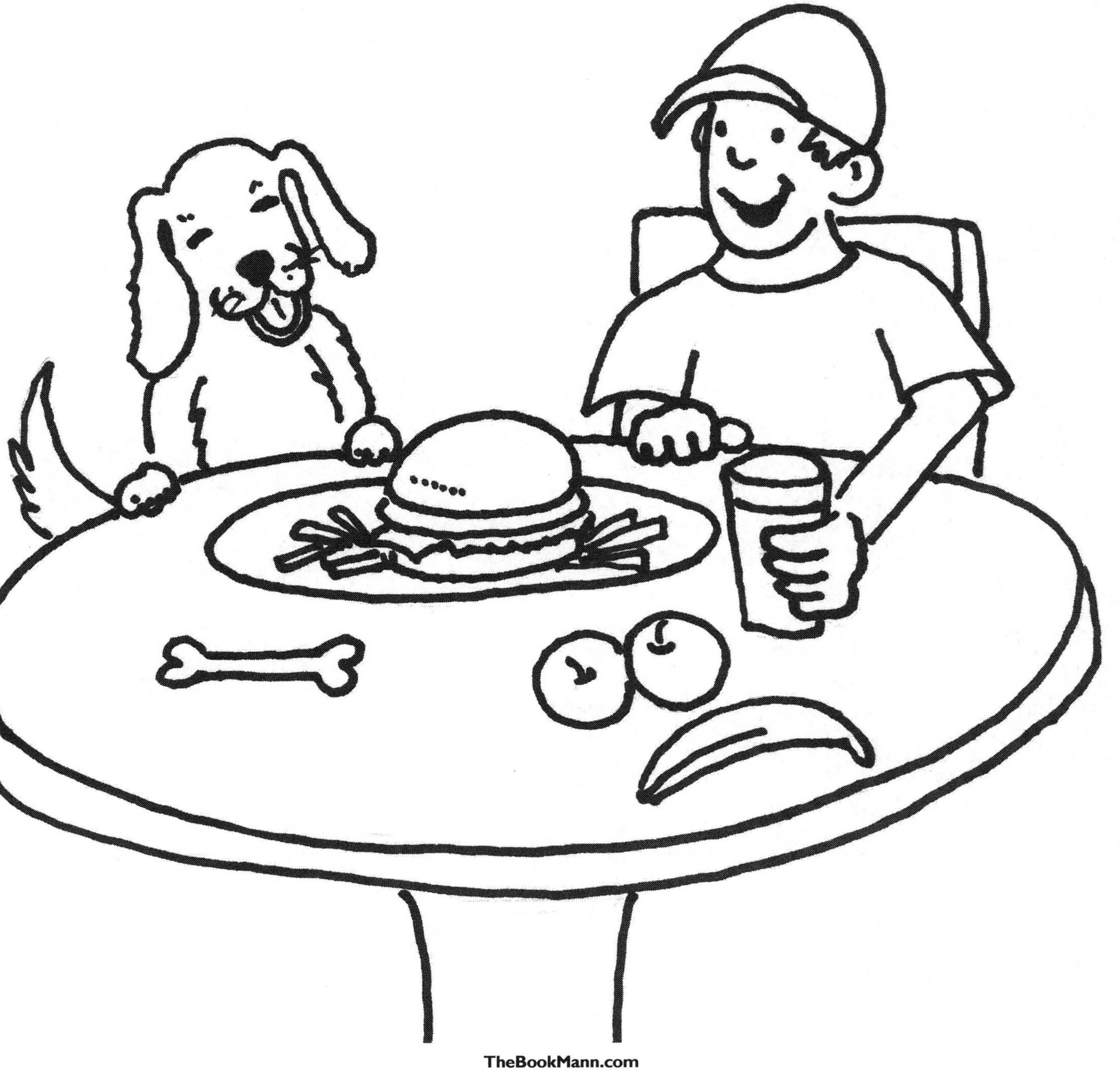

WHERE'S MARVIN?

Find Marvin and his golf equipment hiding in this picture!

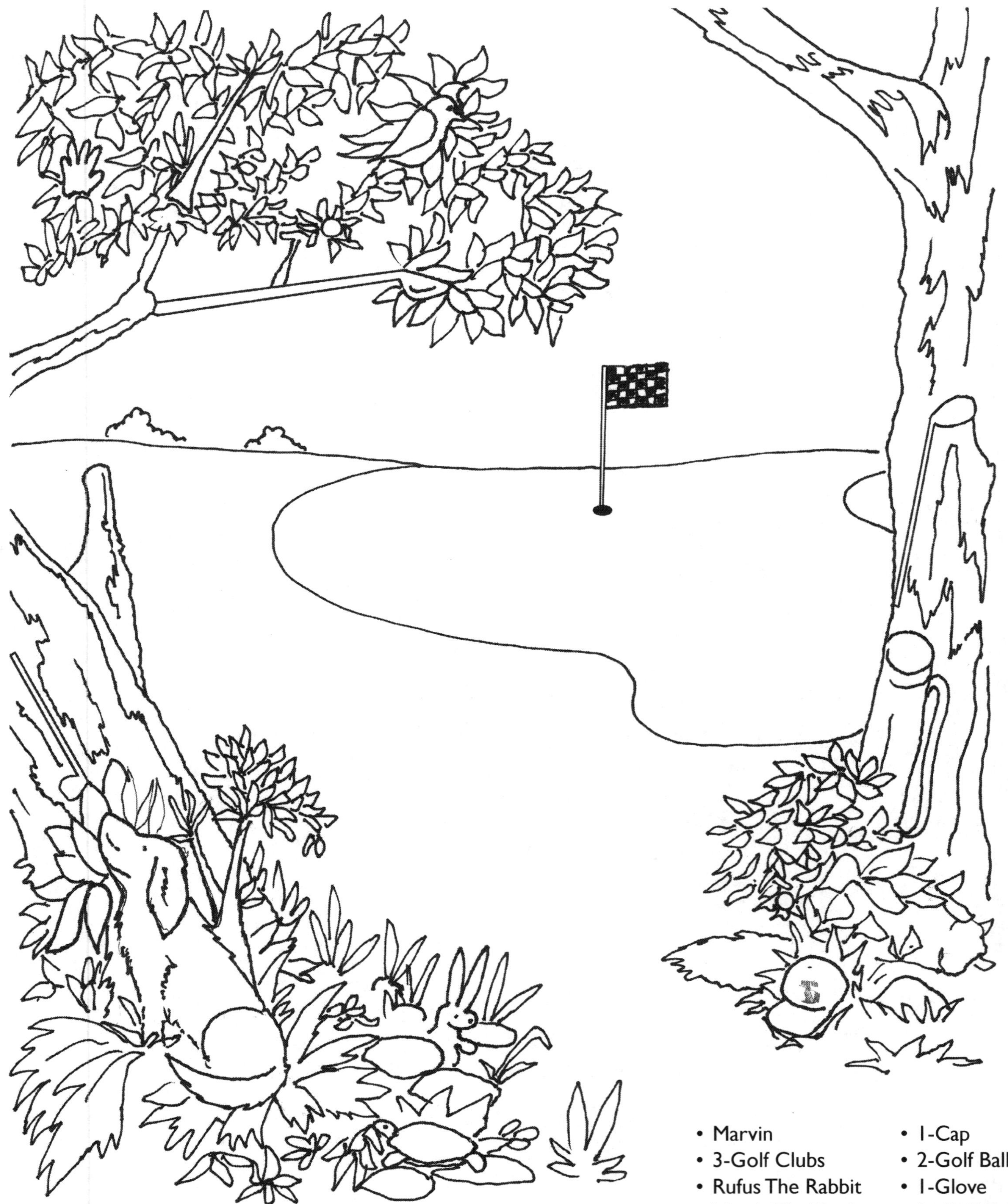

- Marvin
- 3-Golf Clubs
- Rufus The Rabbit
- Myrtle The Turtle
- Henry The Hawk
- 1-Cap
- 2-Golf Balls
- 1-Glove
- 1- Golf Bag
- 1-Tee

MARVIN'S MOST COMMON TERMS FOR GOLF

ZER0	A very good player has a **ZERO** handicap, also known as a scratch golfer.
ONE	There's usually **ONE** golf shop at every course. Check in a half hour before your tee time.
TWO	Begin each hole hitting between the **TWO** tee markers.
THREE	There are **THREE** golf balls in a sleeve.
FOUR	It is ideal to play a round of golf in **FOUR** hours.
FIVE	Be ready to start when you are given a **FIVE**-minute call to the first tee box.
SIX	Ted practices putting to the **SIX** holes on his course's warm-up green.
SEVEN	Ted hits to all **SEVEN** targets on the driving range before teeing off.
EIGHT	**EIGHT** strokes on a hole is called a snowman.
NINE	Most courses are made of two **NINE**s, also called the Front and Back
TEN	A **TEN**-finger grip is how many junior players begin holding a club
ELEVEN	Marvin counted **ELEVEN** tees in the front pocket of Ted's golf bag.
TWELVE	Golf balls come in boxes of **TWELVE**
THIRTEEN	Originally there were only **THIRTEEN** rules to the game of golf – today there are 34!
FOURTEEN	Always check to be sure there are no more than **FOURTEEN** clubs in your golf bag.
FIFTEEN	A ball retriever is also known as the **FIFTEENTH** club
SIXTEEN	Keep hydrated by drinking at least **SIXTEEN** ounces of water
SEVENTEEN	Rule **SEVENTEEN** includes everything you need to know about the Flagstick.
EIGHTEEN	There are **EIGHTEEN** holes in a standard round of golf
NINETEEN	Enjoy a meal after your round in the **NINETEENTH** Hole Café.

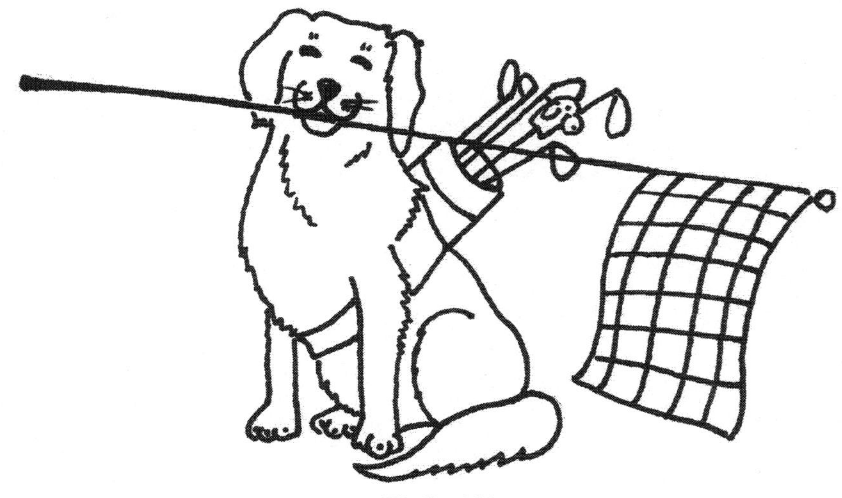

Marvin's Golf Etiquette Tips

- Follow all golf course dress codes. Collared shirts and no jeans.
- Pay attention to any special instructions from the Starter/ Marshall.
- Shake hands with your playing partners before and after the round.
- Stand still and keep quiet while another golfer is hitting the ball or putting.
- Be ready to hit when it is your turn.
- Yell "FORE" if you think your shot may hit someone.
- If you make a divot when striking the ball, always replace or fill with divot mix.
- When on the green, repair your ball mark and any others you see. Sometimes golfers forget.
- Allow the group behind you to play through if your group is playing slow.
- Control your feelings, happy or sad, by taking deep breaths.
- Always leave the course in the great condition you found it.
- It is important to eat and drink during your round, but make sure not to litter.

IF YOU ARE GOOD TO THE GAME,
THE GAME WILL BE GOOD TO YOU!

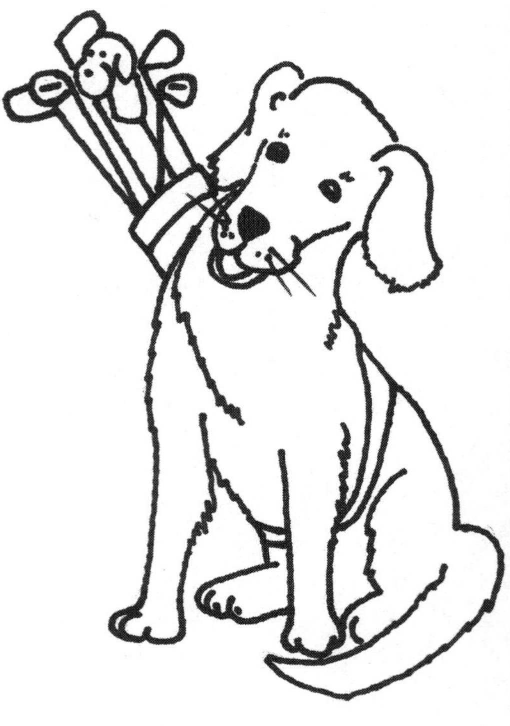